Playtime Prodigies
Season 1 Workbook

ProdigiesMusic.com

By Robert Young

Art & Illustrations By Emma Webb & Rob Young

Edited By Samantha Young

Videos By Jeff Sedwick & Rob Young

Music By Michael Lining & Rob Young

With Art Licensed from FreePik.com

All rights reserved. No part of this publication may be reproduced, stored in a retrieval system, or transmitted by any means without the express permission of Preschool Prodigies and Young Music, LLC.

Published by: Young Music, LLC

ISBN: 978-1-7320173-2-0

Copyright © 2020
Preschool Prodigies and Young Music, LLC
2358 Dutch Neck Road
Smyrna, DE 19977

Prodigies Playground

This Book Belongs To:

_____

Beet & Cherry

Playtime Prodigies

Playtime Prodigies Workbook 3

Let's Draw A Line

To parents: In this activity, your child will practice drawing lines. Guide your child to follow the dotted line with his or her finger. Then, have your child trace the line with a crayon.

Can you help Beet and Cherry get all the way down the page? Trace the lines!

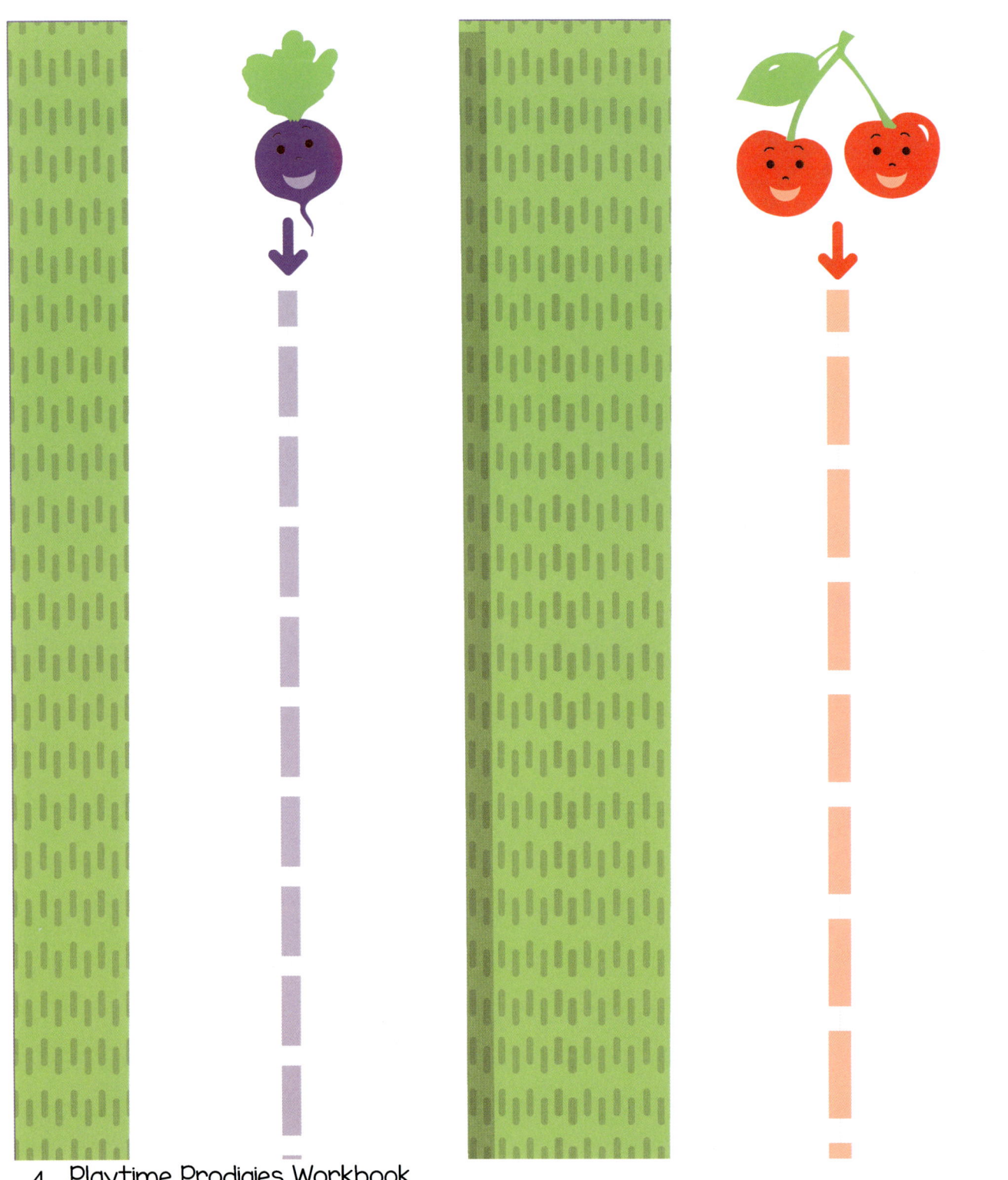

Let's Draw A Line

To parents: In this activity, your child will practice drawing lines. Guide your child to follow the dotted line with his or her finger. Then, have your child trace the line with a crayon.

Can you help Beet and Cherry get across the page? Trace the lines!

Let's Trace the Cherries

To parents: This activity is designed to teach how to draw a circle. Have your child follow the dotted line with his or her finger and then again with a crayon.

Draw a big circle around the cherries.

Let's Tap Together

To parents: Introduce rhythm with some simple tapping on your legs! Tell your child to tap, clap, or stomp along. Cut out the cards below to create a simple rhythm to follow.

Let's tap a steady beat on our legs. Follow along with the Beet cards.

Let's Tap Together (Back)

To parents: Introduce rhythm with some simple tapping on your legs! Tell your child to tap, clap, or stomp along. Cut out the cards below to create a simple rhythm to follow.

Let's tap a steady beat on our legs. Follow along with the Beet cards.

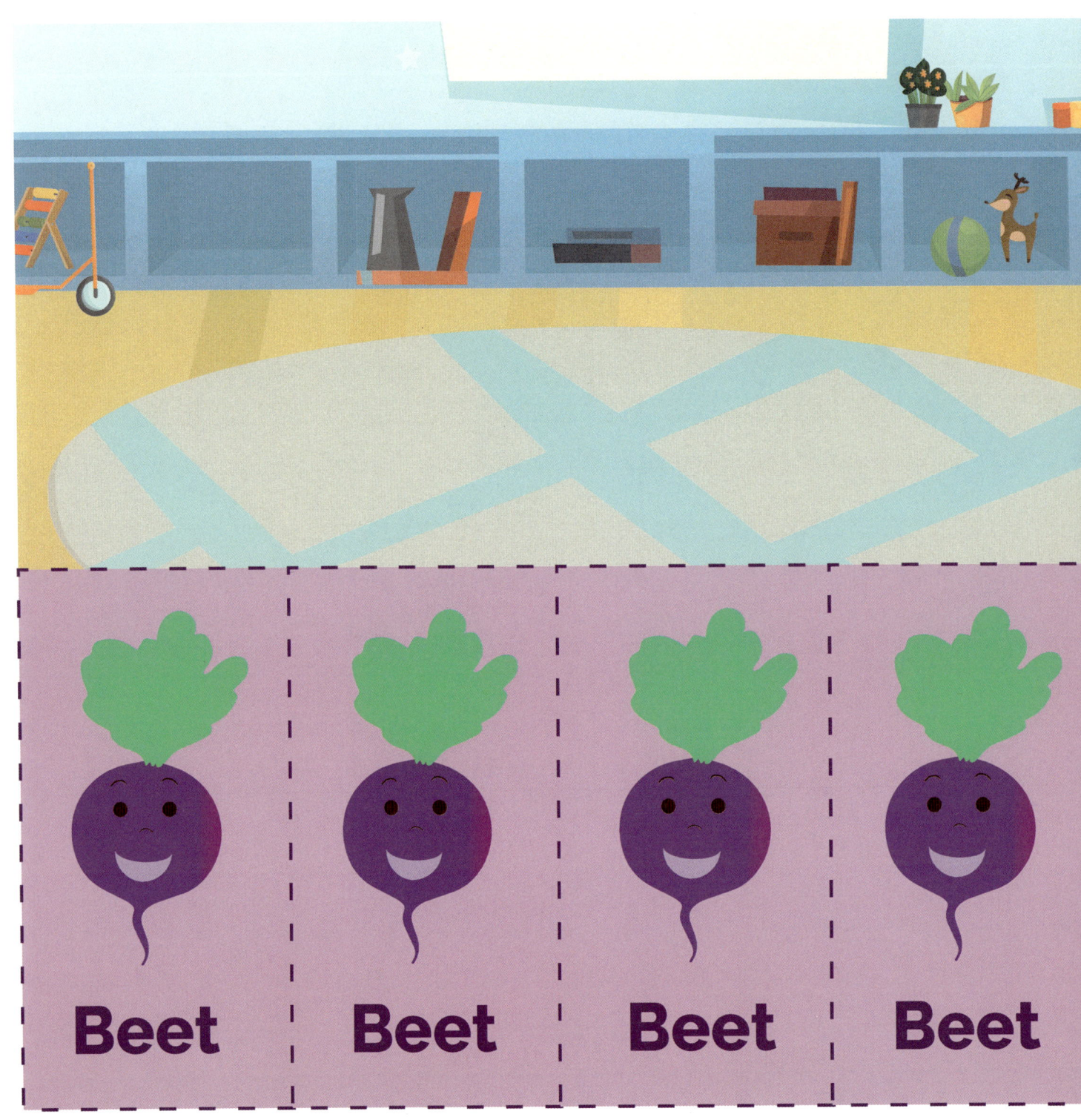

Let's Play With Cherry

To parents: Once your child can tap a steady beat, try playing "beet, beet, cherry, beet." It's okay if it's not perfect at first! Come back and keep practicing. Don't cut out the pieces until the next page.

Can you tap the pattern of "Beet Beet Cherry Beet?" Let's practice!

Playtime Prodigies Workbook 9

Let's Play With Cherry

To parents: Now try Cherry Cherry Beet Beet.
It's okay if it's not perfect at first! Come back and keep practicing.
Then once you're ready, cut out the pieces (double sided) & practice new patterns.

Can you tap the pattern of "Cherry Cherry Beet Beet?" Let's practice!

Let's Find the Fruits

To parents: In this activity, your child will compare and contrast fruits. Ask them to point to the fruit that matches the one in the box. Ask them to explain how they knew which item to pick.

Look at the fruit in the box. Point to the fruit at the bottom of the page that matches the one in the box.

Playtime Prodigies Workbook 11

Campfire Song

Playtime Prodigies

Let's Match the Bells

To parents: After you complete this matching activity, if you have an instrument, play along with each note and point to each bell as you play that note.

Look at the picture in each ◯. Match the faces on the left to the bells on the right. Point or draw a line to connect the pictures.

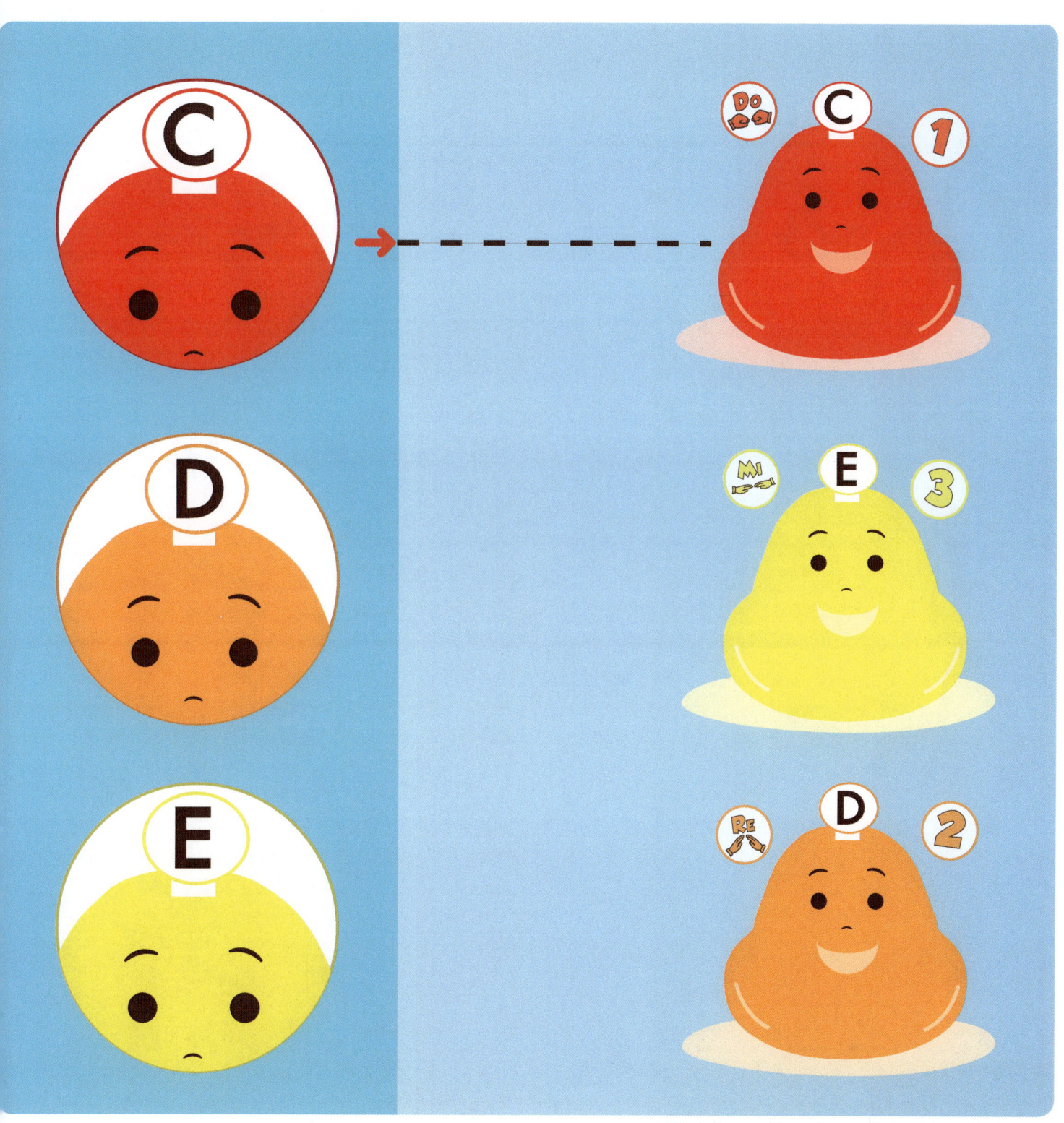

Playtime Prodigies Workbook 13

Let's Draw Lines

To parents: This activity will help your child practice drawing lines from left to right.

Follow the arrow all the way across the page.

14   Playtime Prodigies Workbook

Let's Color the C Bell

To parents: In this activity, your child will practice connecting the color red with the C Bell. Ask them to name something else that is the color red.

Use a red crayon or marker to color the C Bell.

Let's Color the D Bell

To parents: In this activity, your child will practice connecting the color orange with the D Bell. Ask them to name something else that is the color orange.

Use an orange crayon or marker to color the D Bell.

Let's Color the E Bell

To parents: In this activity, your child will practice connecting the color yellow with the E Bell. Ask them to name something else that is the color yellow.

Use a yellow crayon or marker to color the E Bell.

Let's Color the F Bell

To parents: In this activity, your child will practice connecting the color green with the F Bell. Ask them to name something else that is the color green.

Use a green crayon or marker to color the F Bell.

Let's Color the F Bell

Let's Color the G Bell

To parents: In this activity, your child will practice connecting the color teal with the G Bell. Ask them to name something else that is the color teal.

Use a teal crayon or marker to color the G Bell.

Playtime Prodigies Workbook 19

Let's Find What's Red

To parents: In this activity, your child will practice identifying objects that are red. Encourage your child to name the object as they point to each object.

Point to or circle the objects that are red.

Let's Find What's Orange

To parents: In this activity, your child will practice identifying objects that are orange. Encourage your child to name the object as they point to each object.

Point to or circle the objects that are orange.

Let's Find What's Yellow

To parents: In this activity, your child will practice identifying objects that are yellow. Encourage your child to name the object as they point to each object.

Point to or circle the objects that are yellow.

Let's Go Through The Maze

To parents: Explain to your child that this game is called a maze. The object is to connect the Shh bell with the Beet. Explain that in some mazes, it is not clear which way to go. Point out the dead ends in this maze to your child.

Let's help Shh find Beet. Draw a line from Shh to Beet.

Let's Practice Resting

To parents: This activity helps build fine motor control, and reinforces healthy habits like bedtime routines. Encourage your child to sing their favorite bedtime lullaby as they tuck Shh in and create a bedtime routine.

The Shh bell is sleepy!! Can you tuck her in and sing her a bedtime lullaby? What else can we do for her at bed time?

Parents: cut out the blanket for your child

Playtime Prodigies Workbook 25

Let's Practice Resting Back

To parents: This activity helps build fine motor control, and reinforces healthy habits like bedtime routines. Encourage your child to sing their favorite bedtime lullaby as they tuck Shh in and create a bedtime routine.

Let's Shh Together

To parents: Practicing Shh is a fun way to mix up practicing a steady beat. Practice the 4 Shhs in a row below. Then cut the cards out and rearrange them with the cards on the next page to practice some new patterns.

Let's practice Shh together! Can you hold your finger to your lips and make the shush sound?

Playtime Prodigies Workbook

Let's Shh Together (Back)

To parents: Practicing Shh is a fun way to mix up practicing a steady beat. Practice the 4 Shh's in a row below. Then cut the cards out and rearrange them with the cards on the next page to practice some new patterns.

Let's practice Shh together! Can you hold your finger to your lips and make the shush sound?

28 Playtime Prodigies Workbook

Let's Play With Shh

To parents: Now that we've introduced shh, try combining Beet and Shh.
It's okay if it's not perfect at first! Come back and keep practicing.
Then once you're ready, cut out the pieces & practice new patterns.

Can you tap & shh with the patterns below?

Once you've got it, cut out the pieces and make some new patterns.

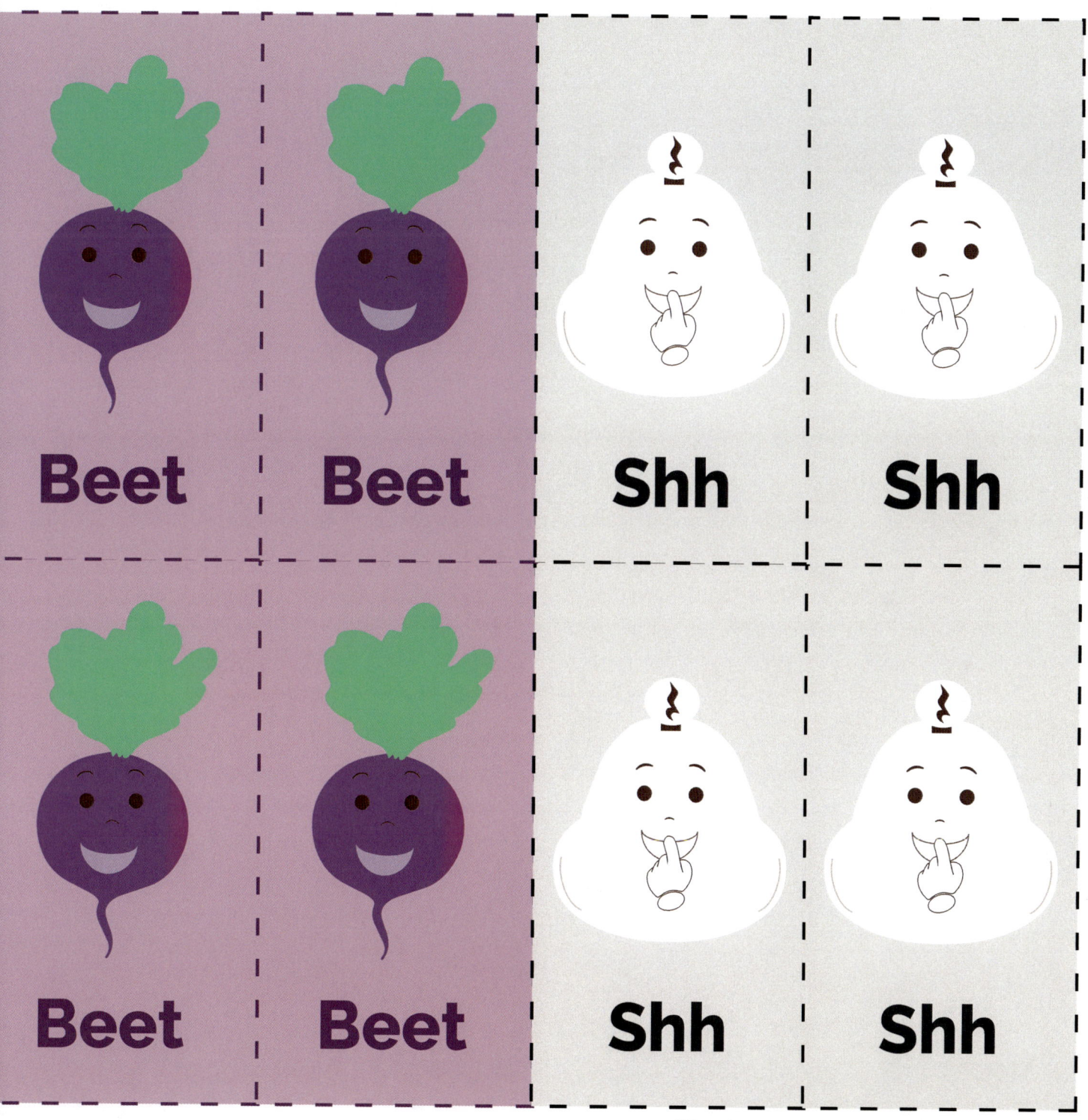

Let's Play With Shh (Back)

To parents: Now that we've introduced shh, try combining Beet and Shh.
It's okay if it's not perfect at first! Come back and keep practicing.
Then once you're ready, cut out the pieces & practice new patterns.

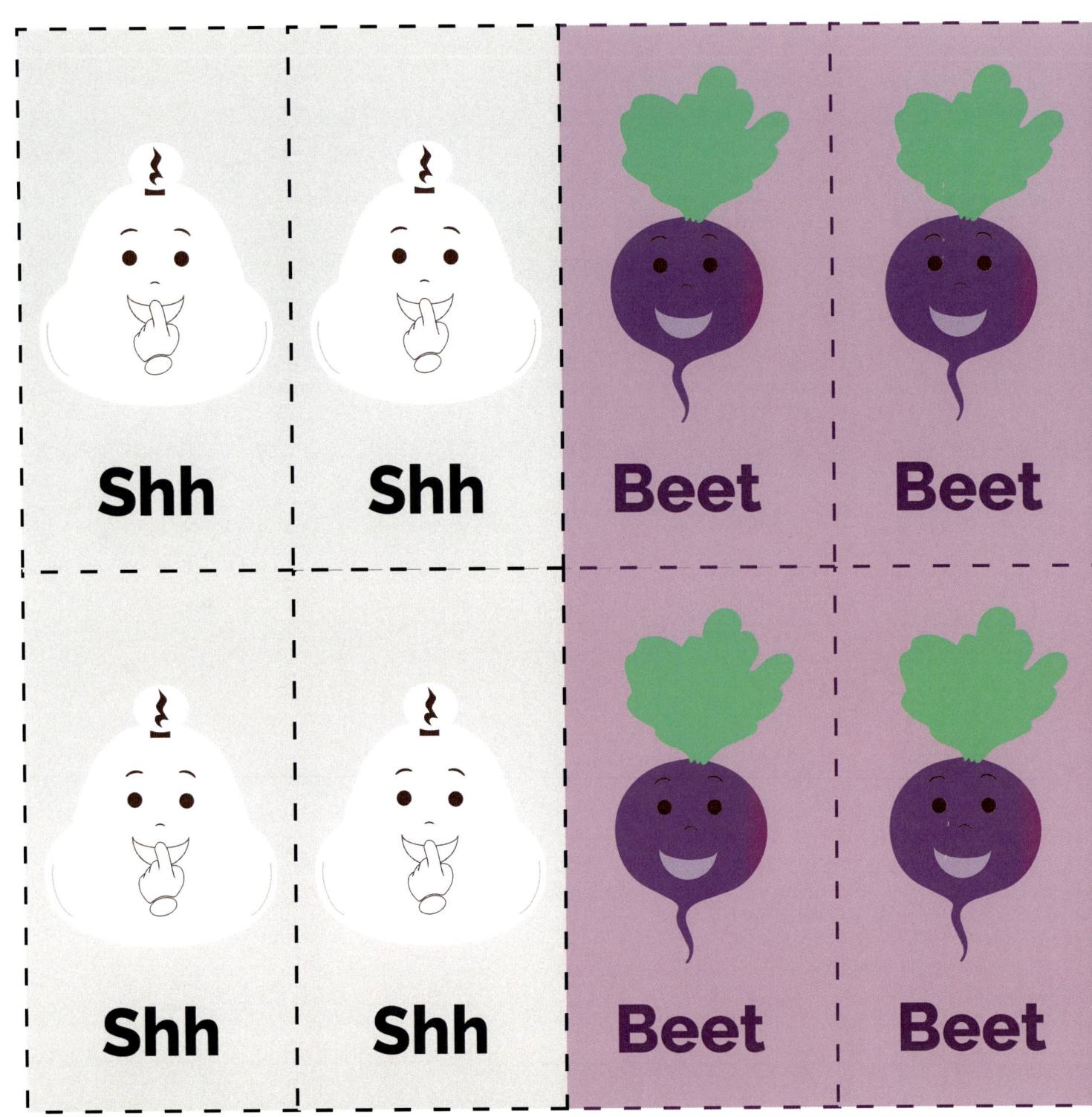

Let's Color the Wagon

To parents: In this activity your child will practice coloring and have a chance to share his or her favorite color. If the color they choose matches one of the C major notes, ask them if they see a bell that matches.

Color the Wagon with your favorite color!

Playtime Prodigies Workbook 31

Vivaldi's Spring
Playtime Prodigies

Let's Have a Performance with E

To parents: It's theatre time!! Cut out the square below. Gently fold the top flap in. Then fold the bottom flap in. Then unfold to make a stage and put the E bell on stage! Encourage your child to make up their own sing using E.

Play or sing with the note E and have a Performance!

Don't forget to take a bow and give yourself a round of applause.

Let's Have a Performance with E

To parents: It's theatre time!! Cut out the square below. Gently fold the top flap in. Then fold the bottom flap in. Then unfold to make a stage and put the E bell on stage! Encourage your child to make up their own sing using E!

Play or sing with the note E and have a Performance!

Don't forget to take a bow and give yourself a round of applause.

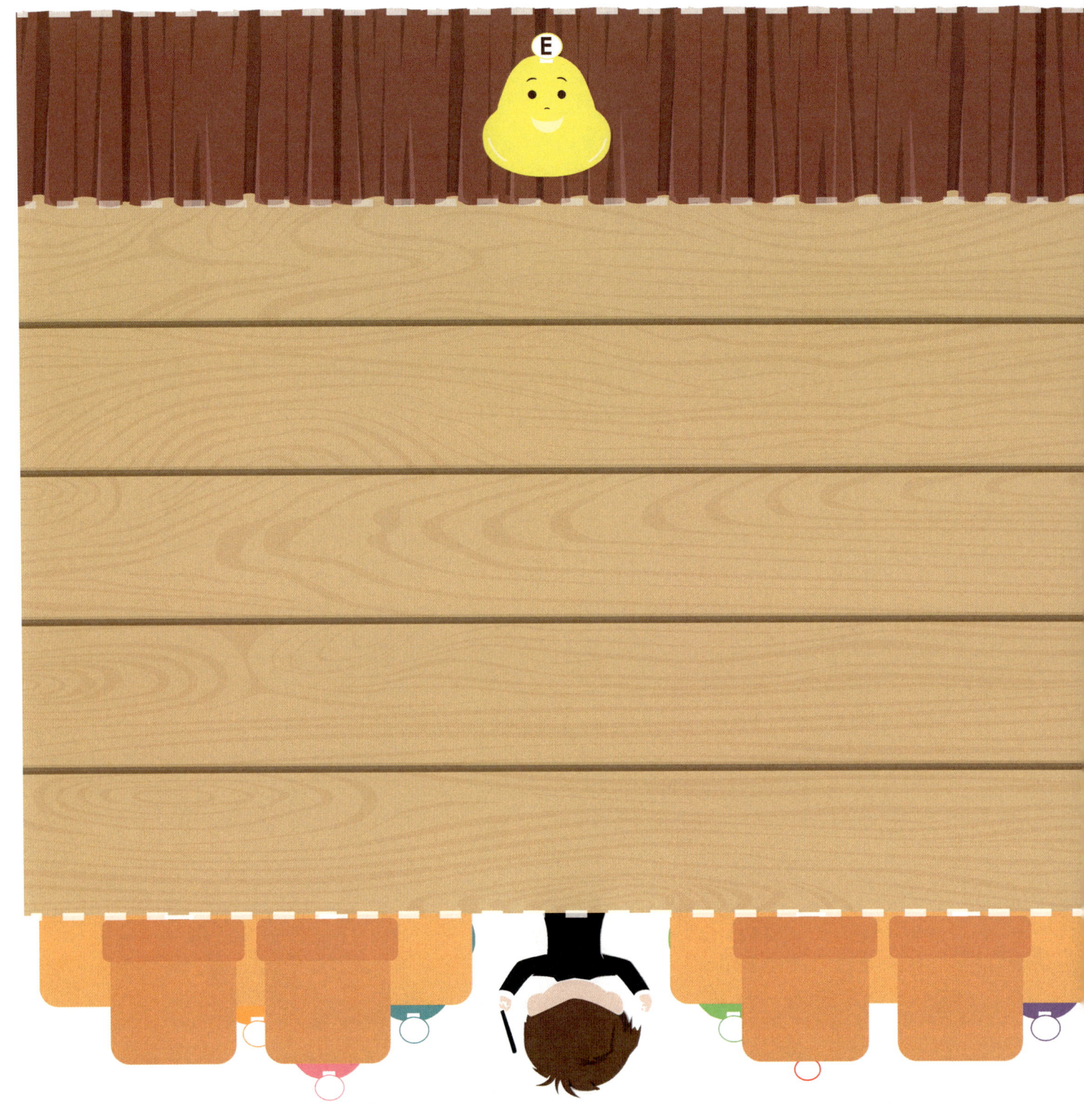

Let's Go Through the Maze

To parents: Mazes help your child look for possible problems or obstacles and then to find ways around them. They improve focus, problem-solving, and fine motor control.

Let's help the sun shine on the garden and help the flowers grow! Trace line from the sun to the flower.

Let's Color With Yellow

To parents: After your child finishes coloring, ask him or her to name each object to practice vocabulary. Make sure that your child only uses the yellow crayon.

Color the objects below with yellow.

Let's Color the Number 1

To parents: In this activity, your child will practice coloring, and connecting the color red with the number 1. After coloring, ask your child to count to 1.

Color the number 1 with a red crayon.

Playtime Prodigies Workbook

Let's Color the Number 2

To parents: In this activity, your child will practice coloring, and connecting the color orange with the number 2. After coloring, ask your child to count to 2.

Color the number 2 with an orange crayon.

Let's Color the Number 3

To parents: In this activity, your child will practice coloring, and connecting the color yellow with the number 3. After coloring, ask your child to count to 3.

Color the number 3 with a yellow crayon.

Playtime Prodigies Workbook

Let's Color the Number 4

To parents: In this activity, your child will practice coloring, and connecting the color green with the number 4. After coloring, ask your child to count to 4.

Color the number 4 with a green crayon.

40   Playtime Prodigies Workbook

Let's Color the Number 5

To parents: In this activity, your child will practice coloring, and connecting the color teal with the number 5. After coloring, ask your child to count to 5.

Color the number 5 with a teal crayon.

Playtime Prodigies Workbook 41

Let's Count to Five

To parents: Practice counting to five with your little one. Next, ask them to name the colors and Solfege names of each number on the rainbow.

What numbers do you see on the rainbow? Say them aloud!

Do Mi Sol

Totigies Teaser

Let's Match Hand Signs

To parents: Have your child connect the Solfege name to the hand-sign by tracing the connecting line. Next, perform each hand-sign.

Connect each Solfege name to the hand-sign.

Let's Practice Signing Do

To parents: Demonstrate the Do hand-sign and explain to your child that this is the hand-sign for Do or C. Then, cut out each card to make a short pattern.

Make the hand-sign for Do.

Playtime Prodigies Workbook 45

Let's Practice Signing Do Back

To parents: Demonstrate the Do hand-sign and explain to your child that this is the hand-sign for Do or C. Then, cut out each card to make a short pattern.

Make the hand-sign for Do.

Let's Practice Signing Re

To parents: Demonstrate the Re hand-sign and explain to your child that this is the hand-sign for Re or D. Then, cut out each card to make a short pattern with the other signs.

Make the hand-sign for Re.

Let's Practice Signing Re

To parents: Demonstrate the Re hand-sign and explain to your child that this is the hand-sign for Re or D. Then, cut out each card to make a short pattern with the other signs.

Make the hand-sign for Re.

48   Playtime Prodigies Workbook

Let's Practice Signing Mi

To parents: Demonstrate the Mi hand-sign and explain to your child that this is the hand-sign for Mi or E. Then, cut out each card to make a short pattern with the other signs.

Make the hand-sign for Mi.

Playtime Prodigies Workbook 49

Let's Practice Signing Mi

To parents: Demonstrate the Mi hand-sign and explain to your child that this is the hand-sign for Mi or E. Then, cut out each card to make a short pattern with the other signs.

Make the hand-sign for Mi.

Let's Practice Signing Fa

To parents: Demonstrate the Fa hand-sign and explain to your child that this is the hand-sign for Fa or F. Then, cut out each card to make a short pattern with the other signs.

Make the hand-sign for Fa.

Playtime Prodigies Workbook

Let's Practice Signing Fa

To parents: Demonstrate the Fa hand-sign and explain to your child that this is the hand-sign for Fa or F. Then, cut out each card to make a short pattern with the other signs.

Make the hand-sign for Fa.

52   Playtime Prodigies Workbook

Let's Practice Signing Sol

To parents: Demonstrate the Sol hand-sign and explain to your child that this is the hand-sign for Sol or G. Then, cut out each card to make a short pattern with the other signs.

Make the hand-sign for Sol.

Let's Practice Signing Sol

To parents: Demonstrate the Sol hand-sign and explain to your child that this is the hand-sign for Sol or G. Then, cut out each card to make a short pattern with the other signs.

Make the hand-sign for Sol.

Let's Match Hand Signs

To parents: Have your child connect the Solfege name to the hand-sign by tracing the connecting line. Next, perform each hand-sign.

Connect each Solfege name to the hand-sign.

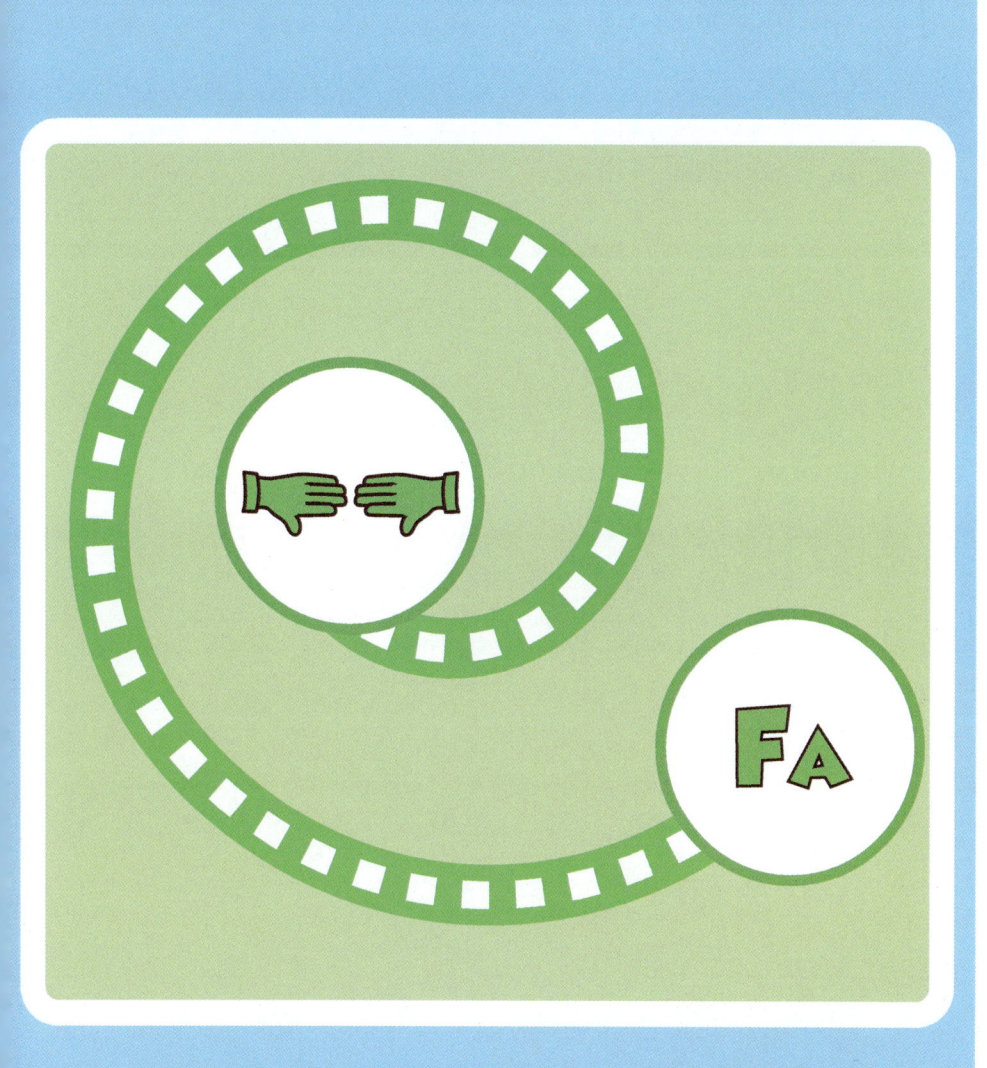

Beet & Melon

Playtime Prodigies

IF YOU WANT SOME SWEET BEETS, WE'VE GOT EM

Who Is Smaller?

To parents: This activity is designed for your child to differentiate between small and large objects. In each box, ask your child to point to the object that is smaller.

Point to the smallest item in each box.

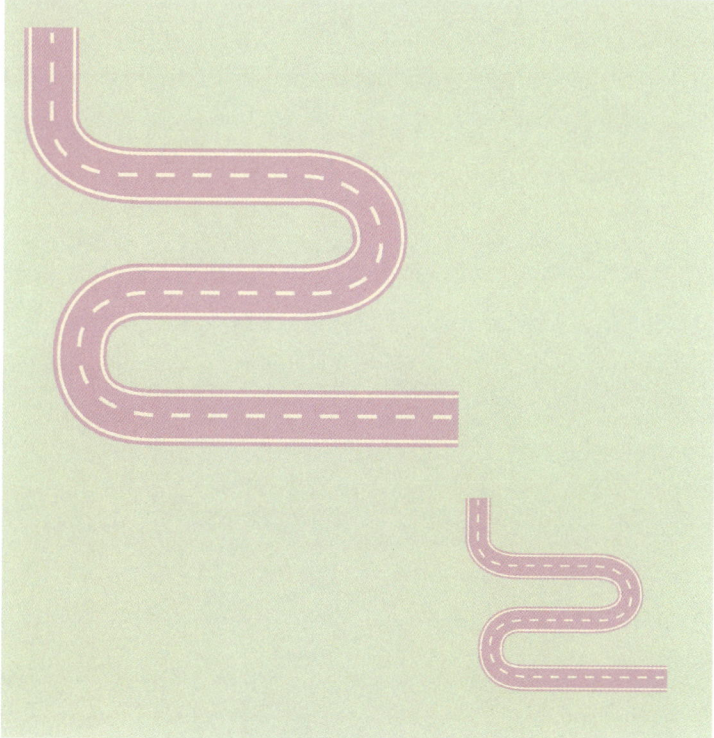

Who Is Smaller?

To parents: This activity is designed for your child to differentiate between small and large objects. In each box, ask your child to point to the object that is smaller.

Point to the smallest item in each box.

58 Playtime Prodigies Workbook

Let's Trace the Beet

To parents: Have your child follow the dotted line with his or her finger and then again with a crayon.

Trace the beet with your finger and then again with a crayon.

Playtime Prodigies Workbook

Let's Color the Fruits

To parents: Use a yellow, green and red crayon to help your child color each fruit with the matching crayom.

Color each white circle to match each fruit.

Let's Draw a Melon

To parents: Challenge your child to draw a circle without tracing a dotted line.

Draw a Line from 🟢→ to 🔴→

Let's Go Through the Maze

To parents: Encourage your child to draw slowly to keep from going off the road the best they can. Mazes help strengthen fine motor skills and improve the ability to think ahead.

Draw a line from Beet to Melon by following the road with your finger or a crayon.

62 Playtime Prodigies Workbook

Let's Tap Together

To parents: Practice tapping with the half note Melons. Half notes get two beats, so tap on the first syllable "Me" and hold the note for "lon". Then cut the cards out and make your own pattern. Combine these cards with those from past pages to create a more complicated rhythm.

Let's practice the half note Melon together!

Me - lon   Me - lon

Playtime Prodigies Workbook 63

Let's Tap Together (Back)

To parents: Practice tapping with the half note Melons. Half notes get two beats, so tap on the first syllable "Mel" and hold the note for "lon". Then cut the cards out and make your own pattern. Combine these cards with those from past pages to create a more complicated rhythm.

Let's practice the half note Melon together!

Me - lon   Me - lon

Let's Play Card Games

To parents: Cut out each card and make your own rhythm using the half note Melons and the quarter note Beets.

Make your own rhythm and tap, clap, or sing along.

Me - lon	Me - lon

Beet	Beet	Beet	Beet

Playtime Prodigies Workbook 65

Let's Play Card Games Back

To parents: Cut out each card and make your own rhythm using the half note Melons and the quarter note Beets.

Make your own rhythm and tap, clap, or sing along.

Me - lon   Me - lon

Beet   Beet   Beet   Beet

66   Playtime Prodigies Workbook

I'm a Nut

Playtime Prodigies

I'm a Nut

VERSE 1

I'm an acorn small and brown

Lying on the cold cold ground

Everybody steps on me

That is why I'm cracked you see

CHORUS

'Cause I'm a Nut

Clap Clap

I'm a Nut

Clap Clap

I'm a Nut (x 3)

Clap Clap

VERSE 2

I called myself up on the phone

Just to see if I was home

I asked myself on a dinner date

I'll pick me up 'bout half past 8

CHORUS

'Cause I'm a Nut

Clap Clap

I'm a Nut

Clap Clap

I'm a Nut (x 3)

Clap Clap

VERSE 3

I'm an acorn small and brown

Flying 'bove the cold cold ground

Nobody can step on me

That's why I sing happily

**CHORUS
(SING TWICE)**

That I'm a Nut

Clap Clap

I'm a Nut

Clap Clap

I'm a Nut (x 3)

Clap Clap

Who Is Smaller?

To parents: This activity is designed for your child to differentiate between small and large objects. In each box, ask your child to point to the object that is smaller.

Point to the smallest item in each box.

Let's Draw an Owl

To parents: Encourage your child to start at the brown arrow and draw the shape of the owl.

Let's draw the shape of the owl. Draw a line from ➡ to ➡

Let's Find Which One is Different

To parents: Help your child determine which animal is different in each row. Point to each animal and ask them to say the color of each one. Then circle the one that is different.

Point to the item that is different in each row.

72 Playtime Prodigies Workbook

Let's Draw a Face

To parents: Ask your child to identify the parts of your face or the parts of the face on the fox on the previous page. Next, ask your child to draw each part on the fox.

Oops! This little fox has lost its face! Can you give this cute fox a face?

Playtime Prodigies Workbook 73

Let's Go Through the Maze

To parents: Have your child stop and study the path before he or she draws a line.

Help the nut float over the clouds and land in the tree! Follow the line with your finger or crayon from the nut to the tree.

Playtime Prodigies Workbook

Beethoven's 5th

Playtime Prodigies

Who Is Smaller?

To parents: This activity is designed for your child to differentiate between small and large objects. In each box, ask your child to point to the object that is smaller.

Point to the smallest item in each box.

Let's Have a Performance with C and G

To parents: It's theatre time!! Cut out the square below. Gently fold the top flap in. Then fold the bottom flap in. Then unfold to make a stage and put the C & G bells on stage! Encourage your child to make up their own sing using C & G.

Play or sing with the notes C & G and have a Performance!

Don't forget to take a bow and give yourself a round of applause.

Let's Have a Performance with C and G (Back)

To parents: It's theatre time!! Cut out the square below. Gently fold the top flap in. Then fold the bottom flap in. Then unfold to make a stage and put the C & G bells on stage! Encourage your child to make up their own sing using C & G.

Play or sing with the notes C & G and have a Performance!

Don't forget to take a bow and give yourself a round of applause.

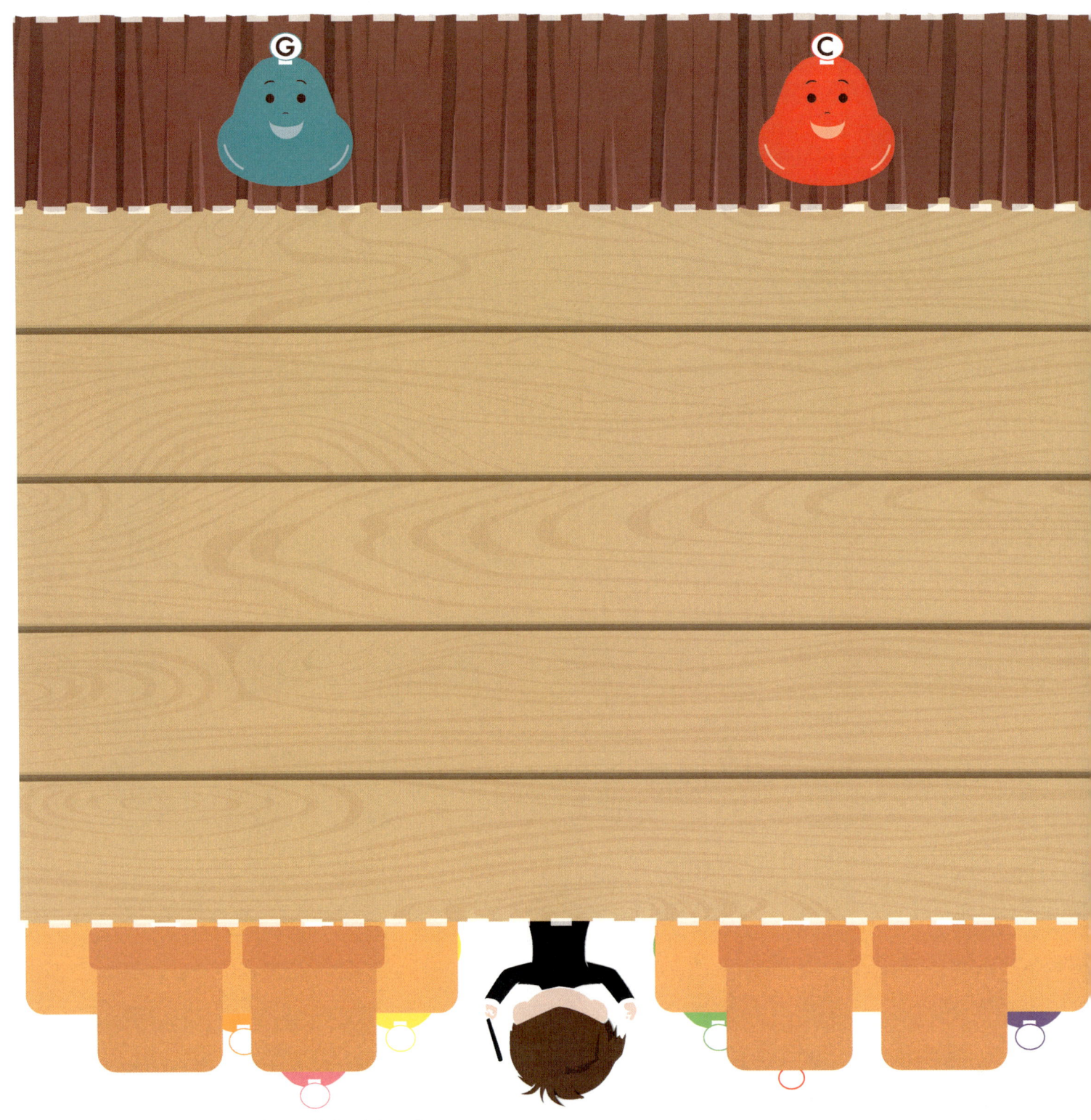

78 Playtime Prodigies Workbook

Who Is Smaller?

To parents: This activity is designed for your child to differentiate between small and large objects. In each box, ask your child to point to the object that is smaller.

Point to the smallest item in each box.

Let's Color the Letter C

To parents: In this activity, your child will practice coloring, and connecting the color red with the letter C. This will help your child memorize the note C.

Use a red crayon or marker to color the letter C.

80 Playtime Prodigies Workbook

Let's Color the Letter D

To parents: In this activity, your child will practice coloring, and connecting the color orange with the letter D. This will help your child memorize the note D.

Use an orange crayon or marker to color the letter D.

Let's Color the Letter E

To parents: In this activity, your child will practice coloring, and connecting the color yellow with the letter E. This will help your child memorize the note E.

Use a yellow crayon or marker to color the letter E.

Let's Color the Letter E

82   Playtime Prodigies Workbook

Let's Color the Letter F

To parents: In this activity, your child will practice coloring, and connecting the color green with the letter F. This will help your child memorize the note F.

Use a green crayon or marker to color the letter F.

Playtime Prodigies Workbook 83

Let's Color the Letter G

To parents: In this activity, your child will practice coloring, and connecting the color teal with the letter G. This will help your child memorize the note G.

Use a teal crayon or marker to color the letter G.

Beet & Watermelon

Playtime Prodigies

Wa – ter mel – on

Playtime Prodigies Workbook 85

Let's Connect Cherries with Beet

To parents: Before your child draws the maze, encourage him or her to examine each path option before deciding which way to go.

Help the Cherries find their friend Beet!

Let's Tap Together

To parents: Practice tapping with the whole note Watermelons. Whole notes get four beats, so either tap on the first syllable and hold the note, or drumroll for the duration of "watermelon". Then cut the cards out and make your own pattern. Combine these cards with those from past pages to create more rhythms.

Let's practice the whole note Watermelon together!

Wa - ter - mel - on

Playtime Prodigies Workbook

Let's Tap Together Back

To parents: Practice tapping with the whole note Watermelons. Whole notes get four beats, so either tap on the first syllable and hold the note, or drumroll for the duration of "watermelon". Then cut the cards out and make your own pattern. Combine these cards with those from past pages to create more rhythms.

Let's practice the whole note Watermelon together!

Wa - ter - mel - on

Let's Play Card Games

To parents: Cut out each card and make your own rhythm using the whole note Watermelon and the quarter note Beets.

Make your own rhythm and tap, clap, or sing along.

Wa - ter - mel - on

Beet   Beet   Beet   Beet

Let's Play Card Games Back

To parents: Cut out each card and make your own rhythm using the whole note Watermelon and the quarter note Beets.

Make your own rhythm and tap, clap, or sing along.

Wa - ter - mel - on

Beet | Beet | Beet | Beet

90 Playtime Prodigies Workbook

Let's Find the Different Fruit

To parents: Ask your child to point to each object and name each one. Then circle the one that is different.

One object is different from the others! Find the object that is different.

Who Is Smaller?

To parents: This activity is designed for your child to differentiate between small and large objects. In each box, ask your child to point to the object that is smaller.

Point to the smallest item in each box.

92   Playtime Prodigies Workbook

Let's Make Fruit Salad

To parents: You'll need a glue stick for this activity! Tell your child to first match each square to the color of the cut-out squares. Once they are matched, have your child glue them in place.

Glue the pieces of fruit to each square to make a fruit salad.

Parents: Cut out the fruit for your child

Let's Make Fruit Salad (Back)

94 Playtime Prodigies Workbook

Let's Make a Cherry Tree

To parents: Your child will practice fine motor control by tearing out cherries from the red strip below. The cherries won't be perfect circles, and that's okay! Then, have your child glue each cherry to the tree below.

Tear the red paper into cherries. Then, glue the cherries onto the tree.

Let's Make a Cherry Tree (Back)

To parents: Your child will practice fine motor control by tearing out cherries from the red strip below. The cherries won't be perfect circles, and that's okay! Then, have your child glue each cherry to the tree below.

Tear the red paper into cherries. Then, glue the cherries onto the tree.

96   Playtime Prodigies Workbook

Let's Go Through the Maze

To parents: Mazes help children strengthen their fine motor skills and improve their ability to think ahead.

Watermelon needs help getting back to Beet! Can you drawn a line from the arrow to the beet?

Meteor Man

Playtime Prodigies

Let's Color the Spaceship

To parents: Encourage your child to color each section of the spaceship a different color. Ask your child if their colors match any of the C Major bells.

Color the Spaceship with your favorite color crayons.

Let's Find The Matching Shape

To parents: Point to each object and ask your child to name it. Then point to the shadow in the box, and ask them to match the shap with one below.

Look at the shadow in the box. Find the picture that matches the shadow. Draw a line to connect the match.

Example

100   Playtime Prodigies Workbook

Let's Count Some Rocks

To parents: Be sure that your child begins at the first red flag, then using your finger, count up to five. Then trace the path with a crayon. Next, challenge your child by asking them to count each rock at each flag.

Help the rocket go through the sky by counting from 1 to 5.

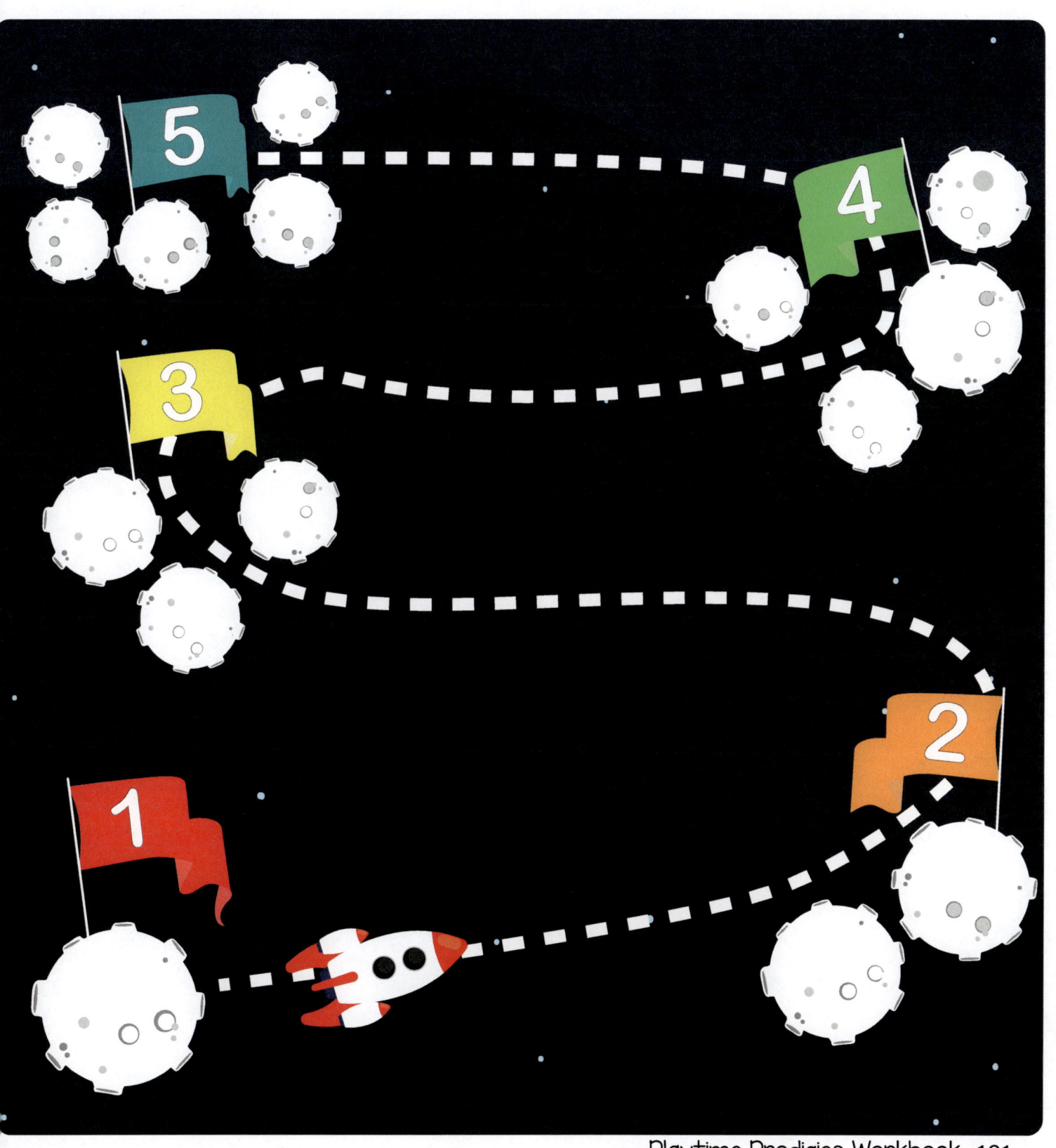

Let's Trace the Earth's Orbit

To parents: Have your child follow the dotted line with his or her finger and then again with a crayon. Start tracing at the right-most arrow all the way around.

Draw a circle around the Earth.

Let's Wear an Astronaut Mask

To parents: Cut out the outer edge of the mask. Use a hole puncher to punch holes on either side indicated by the white dots. Thread a string through holes to tie mask behind child's head.

Wear an Astronaut Mask and pretend you're flying through Outer Space!

Playtime Prodigies Workbook

Let's Wear an Astronaut Mask (Back)

104 Playtime Prodigies Workbook

Let's Color Saturn's Rings

To parents: Practice coloring by filling in the rings around Saturn with any of the colors from the Solfege scale.

Color Saturn's Rings.

Playtime Prodigies Workbook 105

Prodigies Playground
CONGRATULATIONS

You've Completed

Playtime Prodigies
Book 1

Nice work!

_____ _____
Teacher Signature   Date

Made in the USA
Columbia, SC
02 October 2021